Blinding Lights

Cataloging-in-Publication Data
(Publisher)

Menache, Baruch, author.
Blinding lights : poetry / Baruch Menache.
— Fourth edition.
107 pages ; 23 cm

Identifiers:
ISBN 978-1-971928-48-7 (paperback)
ISBN 978-1-971928-49-4 (eBook)

Subjects:
LCSH:
Poetry.
American poetry—21st century.

Classification:
LCC PS3613.E53 B55 2025
DDC 811/.6—dc23

Fourth Edition

McWest & Associates

New York, NY

United States of America

© 2025 Baruch Menache

ISBN: 9781971928487

Blinding Lights

Poetry

by

Baruch Menache

Contents:

Lady Liberty

Choosing Lady Liberty over Lady
Daphery.

As for the rest,

They're of no consequence,

Or so Lady Daphery assured me.

Lady Daphery,

Certainly of late respect,

A social mold where—

Roses aren't red,

Mirrors don't reflect;

Rumblings of town

Or mistress in the plural.

To give soul without return—

Lady Liberty Indeed.

Measurements

Behind the wretched tailor
Sayin' the measurements ain't so.
Scrapping the umbrella holder
For the suit won't be ready in time,
To a wish of a cumbersome maid
That finds me most wretched of all.

Love's Void

We knew each other once,

In another lifetime, that is,

And suddenly, it was you and me;

Space—ashamed at ever showing its vile face.

Love not returned is a shame

How flowers bloom to an empty forest

Or the way memory is lost to wind,

Saving remnants of a last encounter,

That may never be or never was;

Then to the dearly departed

Knowing its absence seeds unraveling.

Days and months make spin

In trade winds and settled seas;

Daybreak, winter-break and the off-season.

Cherished in its time to do the merry

Beholden to a moment of the expected.

Sorrow

Sorrow friended to drink loss;
To the lingering trail of reminders,
To the sensation.
The passing of strangers
To resist a redesign.

Awe

The shooting star arrived late

Too interested in the awe of the
unknown.

Screaming mortality as raindrops settled
for the night.

This life, made for the circle that
faithfully will not lead to a spiral;

Let's not spoil it with oranges.

Trucks

Trucks making stops, routine stops

As cars retake the mirror view.

Fading

The memory, blotted in forgetfulness
A millennium passed on by,
Prickly ordeal—this buried ember.
Take the present to go for your deeds;
Skeletal, forgettable and lonely;
Afraid of the reminder.
To have fallen the grips of nostalgia,
Where a glow perceived an expanse,
More so, the proven case where it was.
Hadn't the expertise to know a fade,
Worse off, raised by two fading figures,
Who were light in a darkness of void.

Drinking coffee remembering our youth
And where and when to find it again.
Shutting windows as the rain creeps in.
The savaged heart knows what it misses
In a dreary sun-laid rapture.

Souls at the beach in a wintery storm,

Always beautiful and full of future,

Wayward to the blossom of summer.

Fairy roses behind a dim lit window

From where do flowers go

Rainbows are there;

Summer and spring,

Youth and old age;

A flower is for all occasions

From which it leads to all places.

The tragedy of a child,

He thinks it will last forever.

Mothers

Collect my feelings for another day.
When skies dimmer to a heartbeat
And children stomp to my pace;
Mothers cradle younglings to hope.

We Need You

We need more photographers at dawn,
More poets in a gripping night,
Artists to tell my wrong,
Corporate to remember my vanity,
Medicine girl to teach my mortality,
Cyber folk to relate to my humanity,
Lovers to help me forget.

We just need more of you all!

The Cold

Warmth had given us strength

To the cold forecast.

Wintery attempts in snow-laden land,

Each return comes with more reluctance.

Never a step forward, tiredly amounted;

Numbing fingers, cold feet and a blushed
face.

These are humans

Foraging for a mortal past.

She smiles, slows her step,

My dear Human!

As I quickly correct the pace,

They didn't see, had they?

Hiding behind layers of warmth,

Unmatched gloves and a fractured spirit;

I see you.

We will meet when the birds return

And have made their nests.

Lost in the Amazon

Lost in the Amazon, it may as well be
New York or Chicago,

Tigers and hyenas, it may as well be the
straphanger,

Each moment—a plan, it may as well be
my schedule,

Tenting in a wilderness, it may as well be
home.

The Calf

Kindly surveying my weakness,
To protect the calf you say.
If I tell you of my need for distance,
It's not that I don't appreciate;
Rather my allotment is more than you
And surely more of my loss of me.

Reflection and Disfavor

They told me to satiate in the drink of
my reflection,

Yonder there, it'll be found.

And so, a young mind,

Path gone forward,

Found I did, and then some.

It was the extra supplications

They didn't want to hear.

To the cave I went

Offering sympathy.

Out I came, promising an extra heart,

They told me in disfavor

All my fragility.

Is it love you see,

Or my disparity?

For I will find some more,

But we know you don't want it.

You will never feel that burden again,

Or each day will be your torment.

The shadow of the sea won't let you
forget,

So wish me goodness,

For I have always done the same.

Crystal Horizon

Lighthearted we walked,
Who is to know a thing like that?
To tell, that it may be ruined.

No! I will not give out,
A mind may never follow.

Sand beneath feet,
Glistening in summer sun
Where the children play;
Crystallite horizon.

Harmony gives laughter a second chance,
Peace—a mantra of yesterday's season.
Daring is the foothold,
Waning to the last edge
Where ripples of currents do no bother,
Singing away the music of yesteryear
With no buffer to the oblivious dusk.

Lonesome Trails

Shoulder to shoulder,

Arm to arm,

No bearing to the lonesome state

Of a user upon a quest.

Surely is its lonesome way

Where valleys meet

And somber fellows reckon lost.

Catching a midnight drift;

Promised nothing.

Must I

Come together.
Why?
Sure you should.
Must I?
It would become of you.
How must I?

This road, back-way entranced,
Where heaven hasn't found
The missing ensemble.

Short of a miracle,
Denounced for promiscuity.
Art, sir, I will make art!

Trust your soul,

Departs before you can find,

Sincerity among beggars

And no-do-gooders.

A braven grievance of relations,

The calming sensation of trouble

That will give you notice of time,

Stolen from the other,

Prior noticed and revealed.

Friends, sir, I will make friends!

Delight in the solitude of misgivings,

Treatment of the earth and its lie,

To dig in place, to become earth,

Never to find more than the husk.

Lilacs at dusk, showers in the evening,

Placing your palm at the edge of this.

Peace, sir, I will make peace!

Build! Such is your might,
Tried and relived,
A Greeks' immortality,
Egyptian oil, Mesopotamia's Jupiter,
Humans walking the Moon.

Sow roots in mother's land,
See yourself alive in the impossible,
Further than foe and friend alike.
Progress, sir, I will make progress!

Summer wills the winter spells,
Trouble chills the calming shores,
Respite gives dear its final touch,
A promise that will never find rest.
Love, sir, I will make love!

To make is to create

That which hasn't time or place,

Must find another way,

Onto dirt paths and hilly roads.

Your journey to do all and in-between,

Until it finds you and bites the bitter.

Depart from you, sir, I will make my
own!

Sophisticated Emptiness

Sophisticated emptiness,

Unregulated brokenness—

Ingredients I've come to know.

You may go down

To remove fabrication

But I warn you—

Another awaits just the same.

"He goes with the wind," they say;

He goes otherwise.

The Empty Promise

We treaded the in-between,
Always marking our progress
And those surround,
Beyond and before.

The afterlife has been solved
On dutiful ground
To circumvent broken beauty.

What if I were to commit to tragedy,
To give myself to imagination
And simulate the experience?

What else? To be a part of this faction?
They place me at their lowest seat.
To work and live will I fulfill
In the emptiness of dreams;
Those that will not leave the kitchen
And its martyrdom.

Causality of being won't endure
Another mark of this bygone,
Of a work from another time
To another page
Of a book burning to come.

I'd rather empty stillness
Of a promised afterlife
Where roses are red
And color has meaning.
A millennium in rainbow
To forget its tainted rue,
And the off-shine that comes with time.

To a grandstanding entrance
Of the abodement of hell.
Devilish in kind
To my fair skin,
Remaining in-trance of
Fumes of kitchen odor.

For the afterlife has been chosen
By life itself.
To commit before execute,
To succeed before trial.

Affirmations to keep alive
As I tread the oblivion.
We tie roots of sadness
And empty waste of urge,
Where going is but for a moment,

The unsolvable life and its misgivings.

Sorry Dear

Dashing mascara—smoked,
Sensible fingers—suited.
Silent treatment, effective glow,
Chimera and excellence.
As the moment cascades the void,
Validating hearts and souls
Before sleep claims her eyes.

Sorry dear, this is a private affair
Where those who made entry
Reluctantly are beholden
While those who wish
Are ill-advised.

Sadly they visit in the rain
With granulated fame.
No dear, mustn't ya wish entry,
Let those within come to you.

You Over There

Hey, you over there,

Have you found solace?

With an abridged version—

What is it you find?

In dark alleys and midnight pubs,

Trucking through a midday section

Of April Showers and Autumn Leaves.

Why is it that I meet you apart from July?

Why is it that I treat you as—
extraterrestrial?

We apologize and show tears,

We make amends and sew bridges.

Isn't that funny?

How resentment stays,

Never touching under the weight of tears

And the sentiment of gold.

Am I asking too much?

Do I pledge against your humanity,

Or to redefine it?

Corner

Corner the page of that yellow,

Shining red, illuminating green.

A grass-bed for all to tell

Of a colorless composite yet serene.

A display apt the heart's content,

Free at last in nature's grace.

To continue, succulent and true

In a method tried by time.

To Thank

Haven't they told you? It should have arrived,

arrived,

Long ago where addresses are found.

To thank the end of way,

To please the entrance,

To the in-between.

Find merry, save for joy,

To retrieve the unfounded

And make do.

Tend to The Dandelions

Tend to the dandelions,

I to the changing shifts,

You to the flowers,

I to the task

Us to the longing.

Color Me

Color me so

With that ribbon bow.

Trouble me a radical

With that cradle toe.

Bridle me a rebel

With that angry foe.

Circle me a social man

With justice as my know.

Color me envious,

Charge me for whatever the crime.

A Clump of Steel

A clump of steel

Will always be a clump of steel.

However you galvanize,

Even of that stainless steel,

It will always be a clump of steel.

I said, deny, deny, deny,

Tell them a story if you must.

Do not give them more than they ask.

Ask them to show you the door

Before the hinges break off

And the bolts fall into place.

Winter Peaks

The cold winter is upon us
For they condone our separation
And wonder about cherry blossoms—
If they even or ever exist.

Trailing superstardom.
Crying on mountain tops, "It's mine,"
Holding dear to mountains deep,
Saying, "This is the only mountain."

Memory

Tasked to extract a memory
To counter the other
And be on our merry way.

Who can count peace
On fingers faced in?
To count love
On fingers faced out?

Profess I will,
Envious or curious,
Trusting to partake the luncheon,

Yet, I haven't divulged my task
Which can destroy just the same.

A Hollow Branch

An escaped hollow branch
Under by Merry Lane,
By the wicket fence
And yellow flag.

To await the day
The smart fellow
Would say no more to—
Merry Lane, its fence, yellow flag
And hollow branch.

Awake for Days

Treading strands of strength
To expand in the sweltering sun,
To see the horizonless.

To need is a closed door—
Sand, dirt, and earth.
Salivating the primrose,
Overstepping consumption,
Dietary of that exiled mammal;
Feral man's lost memory,
Screaming a name alas!
From a demented mind.

Prose of Yesterday

We can go to the prose of yesterday

Written in history books,

Words quoted far too long.

We'd do better at the doorpost,

Reaping words

That hadn't a glance or reprieve.

Drawing Room

A Tuesday morning
Before the coffee break,
The turn of the millennium,
Sent back to the drawing room.

The Duke

The duke on his first day—
That gleaming sword;
Mother is proud.
Only one heart is full;
The returned veteran.

Summer Swells

Summer swells in open wells,
Deserters' to changing beauty.

Ten lasted round three,
Unbeknownst to the cumbersome maid
Who wipes the window sill all the same.

You People

Oh, you poetry people,

Stop being so good.

We mustn't keep to ourselves.

The poet who doesn't flow life's
offerings,

To embrace all with grace and demise.

This poet who has skipped the torture

Will miss a step in the dance of light.

This haven, stolen,

Might we earn it,

So that we can clean our guilt.

The poetic moment is one which

Doesn't reach into anybody's pocket.

Come what may on this golden day,

Between the etches of wooden shaft

And mechanical steel above,

A glimmer of sunlight is still seen.

I celebrate the poetic stream

Of a steady seam,

On this magical encounter

With the end-of-day serene.

Welling Worker

Received by the welling worker,
As strangers stroll on by—
Oh, but a time
Where the stranger receives
And the welling worker looks on;
With envy, with distaste.

She must go now,
He, to his place,
Her, to the pressing call
Of the gliding shifts in Arctic peaks.

The sun sets upon all happenstance.
Quiet, I say,
We will wait another day.

A Performative Walk

A performative walk
In the underground tunnel,
Facial dance of subtle talk.

"This way," says the sign,
"Follow by noon."
The corner alley swiftly marked
While Suburbia is without a map.
Those lovers, a fabric of its walls,
Watching revolution avoid the gate.
It may just be me… in the city.

Those Leaves

Bang those barren leaves,

Extract its water

For my olive trees.

Salvage a crescent moon

On that pale face,

For the sun rises again.

Sanity

Shower rainbows, clemency to my rein
of narrow spaces.

Widened and opened, where weed
bushes grow plenty and I am on the
verge of insanity.

I choose sanity in a midnight winter
solstice;

As the dominant philosophy

Being found on lips of those

On their way to the psych ward.

Survivor or victim,

Refugee of my own heart.

Until What End

The rough patio and smell of roses
Which takes no notice.

The iron fences and woodwork—
Too strong for their defenses,
As we say goodbye to history.

The sacrifice is never clean;
The unsacrificed never stable.
Until what end, I say,
Until what day shall this be on display?

Past June, before summer?
When old age grips us so?
When the dust of the chandelier
And window sill stays put.

More

The heaping and hissing
Of time interloping,
Until a moment in nights' fresh air.
New moon, sorrow and mistakes,
Beginnings and ends, to all for all.

Arriving late into the night,
Gone first thing in the morning;
Something tells me more.

Pagans of the Heart

To fill pagans of heart
With unresolving desperation.

The hidden knowledge
Behind dreary eyes
And a belated heart.

That Voice

That voice,

Society and its demands.

Is it father?

The politeness of mother?

Hovers,

More intimately than lovers.

Who speaks for it?

Do I get my turn to speak back?

Beauty

To fight the wrong,
She was too wise for distractions.

Love will die with contempt;
Strife only brings her lover closer.

Cinderella keeps beauty with sealed lips
And a broken heart.

Opened The Gates

When they opened the gates
I was all in.
When they told me the step,
I followed.
To adhere to its laws,
To its traditions
I went—
The social demands,
Whatever it took.

The Era

Dark spring in her procession—
A moment, if but a moment we knew.

Awe and subtle was her name,
Before twenty others came along.

The forgotten tone of our pace,
Lost in its intertwinings.
We knew the fault and its remedy.

Wipe your lips of a misstep;
No memory will be observed.

Daughter of Modernity

She became confused.
Who is to blame her so?
So did I, in my love for thy.

In 2016, I sought her out,
A year of respite and delight,
Only for her to refuse and deny.

"Forget that," we said,
Until she brings us
Back to life.

A daughter of modernity,
The crime of not asking questions,
The offense rather grave.

When shall she speak again?
Will she perish into the void
Before I turn my back on her?

The Mother Bird

The mother bird,

Kin warm,

Branches and scraps;

Its evolutionary member.

Sit, she will—

Nothing will retract

The mother from mothering the
othering.

A home in nature, a dwelling for nurture.

Can we reside as still

In the abode of a mother bird?

The Cave

I wanted progress
And progression was my aim.

History was on my side,
That was skipped too,
Until I was informed of impotence,
And I went back into the cave.

Ghost

Actions embody me,
Walking earth on my behalf.
Fear in the populace
Shows face at night.

Hidden in the shadows,
Makes some insane, others deranged.
Beyond memory it treads,
Remains quite right under your bed.
My ghosts are alive and well,
Even beyond my own farewell.

The Shadow

Words somber on my lips,

Engaged in all its fruitlessness.

Ashamed, afraid, and lonely—

Oh, so lonely, all gone into another
world,

As I persist the shadow that I thought
light.

Departure

And so it was,

When she took her leave from the
palace,

The last servant of a dying kingdom.

Dust will arrive shortly,

The garden will overgrow.

Laughs and drama subside,

Buried into a past,

Till the adventurer seeks her out

And places her name in history.

Olive Tree

Does it want the merciless plucking of its
fruit,

The angry smacking in the morning sun,

The thrusting of machine,

The delight of men in their quench of
liquid,

The late summer strip of nakedness and
bare?

What does an olive tree want?

About the Author

Baruch Menache writes at the intersection of narrative, philosophy, and lyric expression. His work spans poetry, essays, and theatrical pieces that examine the interior life and its many thresholds. He lives in New York with his Wife and Children.